the official
driving test

London: The Stationery Office

Published by The Stationery Office for the Driving Standards Agency under licence from the Controller of Her Majesty's Stationery Office

© Crown copyright 2001.

Applications for reproduction should be made in writing to
The Copyright Unit, Her Majesty's Stationery Office,
St Clements House, 2–16 Colegate, Norwich NR3 1BQ

This title was formerly known as *Your Driving Test*

First edition Crown copyright 1990

Second edition Crown copyright 1993
Third edition Crown copyright 1996
Fourth edition Crown copyright 1999
Fifth edition Crown copyright 2001
Second impression 2001
ISBN 0 11 552254 9

A CIP catalogue record for this book is available from
the British Library

Other titles in the Driving series

The Official Theory Test for Car Drivers

Driving – the Essential Skills

The Official Theory Test for Motorcyclists

Motorcycle Riding – the Essential Skills

The Official Motorcycling – CBT, Theory & Practical Test

The Official DSA Guide for Driving Instructors

The Official Theory Test for Drivers of Large Vehicles

Driving Buses and Coaches – the Official DSA Syllabus

Driving Goods Vehicles – the Official DSA Syllabus

The Official Theory Test for Car Drivers and Motorcyclists (CD-ROM)

The Official Guide to Tractor and Specialist Vehicle Driving Tests

The Official Guide to Accompanying 'L' Drivers

Every effort has been made to ensure that the information contained in this publication is accurate at the time of going to press. The Stationery Office Limited cannot be held responsible for any inaccuracies. Information in this book is for guidance only.

The Driving Standards Agency would like to thank Sterling Motors and FOCALPOINT of Norwich for their kind co-operation in securing the photograph for the front cover.

ii

The Driving Standards Agency (DSA) is an executive agency of the Department for Transport, Local Government and the Regions (DTLR).

You'll see its logo at test centres.

DSA aims to promote road safety through the advancement of driving standards, by

- establishing and developing high standards and best practice in driving and riding on the road; before people start to drive, as they learn, and after they pass their test
- ensuring high standards of instruction for different types of driver and rider
- conducting the statutory theory and practical tests efficiently, fairly and consistently across the country
- providing a centre of excellence for driver training and driving standards
- developing a range of publications and other publicity material designed to promote safe driving for life.

As a Trading Fund, we are required to cover our costs from the driving test fee. We do not have a quota for test passes or fails and if you demonstrate the standard required, you will pass your test.

DSA Website

www.driving-tests.co.uk

DTLR Green Issue Website

www.environment.detr.gov.uk/greening/index.htm

CONTENTS

Each year nearly one million people decide they want to learn to drive a car. You and most of the others will go on to take the driving tests.

The purpose of the tests is to prove that you can drive your vehicle safely on the road. Therefore, it's vitally important to develop the correct attitude towards driving, showing responsibility and consideration to other road users. Only those who can do this will earn the right to drive without L-plates (or D-plates in Wales) and on motorways.

By passing your tests you will have proved that you have learned the theory, but it's important that you understand the principles of what you have learned and put them into practice. The instruction you receive before the tests is the foundation for gaining further skills and experience. The tests are just one stage in your driving career. You shouldn't assume that if you pass your tests you are a good driver with nothing more to learn.

During your practical test your examiner will want to see you driving to the standards set in this book. Those standards are given here in an easy-to-read style with illustrations, which explain simply what is required. However, driving is never predictable. Road conditions or circumstances will demand that you use your initiative or common sense. You should be able to assess any situation and apply the guidance given in this book to it.

Make sure that your aim is *'Safe driving for life'*.

Robin Cummins

The Chief Driving Examiner
Driving Standards Agency

This book will help you to

- learn to drive competently
- prepare and help you to pass your practical driving test.

Part One tells you what you need to do before the test.

Part Two gives the test requirements, with simple, clear advice. Refer to it regularly and use it to check your progress.

Part Three shows what is required if you need to take a test to tow a trailer.

Part Four gives details about the extended test for disqualified drivers.

Part Five contains the official syllabus for learning to drive and lists the skills you need to learn before taking your test. Refer to it regularly.

The important factors

This book is only **one** of the important factors in your training.

The others are

- a good instructor
- plenty of practice
- your attitude.

You must manage your own learning.

Aim to be a safe and confident driver for life, and not just to pass your test.

Driving is a life skill.

Your driving tests are just the beginning.

To help you study

Books

It's strongly recommended that you study a copy of *The Highway Code*. You can buy one from a good bookshop.

The DSA Driving series of books will provide you with sound knowledge of driving skills.

The Official Theory Test for Car Drivers

Driving – the Essential Skills

The Official Guide to Accompanying 'L' Drivers

Other media

The Driving Test – Inside View 2 is a video which explains what the examiners expect to see and gives some practical preparation methods.

What if? is a video and workbook based training programme designed to boost your hazard awareness and your ability to avoid accidents.

The Official Theory Test for Car Drivers and Motorcyclists (CD-ROM) provides an interactive way of learning. You can also practise taking a mock theory test.

All the above are available from good bookshops, or can be purchased direct by telephoning 0870 241 4523.

Part One

Before your test

This part looks at how to prepare yourself for the test.

The topics covered

- The theory test
- About the driving test
- Preparing for your driving test
- Completing a log book
- How to apply for your test
- Before attending your driving test.

Before you take your practical driving test you will have to take a theory test. If you pass that you will be given a pass certificate. You must take this with you when you attend your practical test.

A contractor conducts theory tests on behalf of DSA. There are over 150 theory test centres in Great Britain and Northern Ireland. Theory test sessions are available during weekdays, evenings and on Saturdays. If you wish to book a test, an appointment will be available for you within about two weeks (a bit longer if you have special needs).

You can find out where your local centre is from

- your Approved Driving Instructor (ADI)
- a practical driving test centre
- the telephone information line 0870 01 01 372.

Study your copy of *The Highway Code* and the publication *The Official Theory Test for Car Drivers* (both published by The Stationery Office).

If you are well prepared you won't find the questions difficult. *The Official Theory Test for Car Drivers* will provide you with the questions and answers.

It's very important that you know why the answers are correct. Take this knowledge and put it into practice on the road. Your examiner will expect you to demonstrate what you have learned through your driving.

The driving test is straightforward

You will pass if you can show your examiner that you can

- drive safely
- complete the set exercises
- demonstrate, through your driving, that you have a thorough knowledge of *The Highway Code.*

Does the standard of the test vary?

No. All examiners are trained to assess tests to the same standard.

Test routes are designed and approved locally to include a range of typical road and traffic conditions.

Are the examiners supervised?

Yes, they are closely supervised. A senior officer may sit in on your test.

Don't worry about this. The senior officer won't be examining you, but making sure the examiner is testing you properly. The senior officer won't interfere with the test, so just carry on as if he or she wasn't there.

Can anyone accompany me on the test?

Yes, your instructor or a friend can be present during the test but must not take any part in it.

You should bring an interpreter with you if you need one, but you must not use an Approved Driving Instructor (ADI) for that purpose. Anyone accompanying a driver on a test must be 16 years or over and wear a seat belt if one is available.

Can I use an automatic car for the test?

Yes. When you pass your practical test your full driving licence will entitle you to drive an automatic car. It will also act as a provisional licence for a car with a manual gearbox.

What will my examiner want from me?

Your examiner will want you to drive safely and competently in various road and traffic conditions.

You will be

- given directions clearly and in good time
- asked to carry out set exercises.

Your examiner wants you to do well and will try to put you at your ease. You may wish to talk to your examiner during your test, and in this case she or he will talk with you, but will try to keep this to a minimum because it might put you off.

How should I drive during the test?

Drive in the way that your instructor has taught you.

If you make a mistake, don't worry, keep calm and concentrate on your driving.

How long will the test last?

About 40 minutes.

Note. The extended test for persons convicted of serious offences will last approximately 70 minutes (see Part Four).

What if I do something dangerous?

If at any time during your test your examiner considers you to be a danger to other road users your test won't continue. Prepare yourself and wait until you reach the standards set in this book before you take your test.

What will the test include?

Apart from general driving, your test will include

- an eyesight test (if you fail this, your test won't continue)
- special exercises. You'll be asked to carry out two of the following

- reversing around a corner
- turning in the road
- reverse parking.

You may also be asked to carry out an emergency stop exercise.

What about the special exercises?

The special exercises will take place at carefully selected places.

Your examiner will ask you to pull up, explain the exercise and ask you to carry it out.

What if I don't understand?

Listen carefully to the explanation, but if you aren't sure about anything, ask. Your examiner understands that you may be nervous and won't mind explaining again.

What's the purpose of the test?

The driving test is designed to see if you

- can drive safely
- know *The Highway Code* and can demonstrate this through your driving.

How your driving test is assessed

Your examiner will assess any errors you make and, depending on their degree of seriousness, record them on the Driving Test Report form (DL25). You will fail your test if you commit a serious or dangerous fault. You will also fail if you commit more than a fixed number of driving faults (previously known as minor faults).

The criteria the examiner will use are as follows

Driving fault – less serious, but has been assessed as such because of circumstances at that particular time. An accumulation of driving faults may result in a fail. Accumulating more than 15 driving faults will entail failure.

Serious fault – recorded when a potentially dangerous incident has occurred or a habitual driving fault indicates a serious weakness in a candidate's driving.

Dangerous fault – recorded when a fault is assessed as having caused actual danger during the test.

At the end of the test you will be offered some general guidance to explain your Driving Test Report.

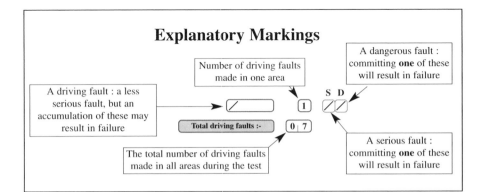

Explanatory Markings

Number of driving faults made in one area

A dangerous fault : committing **one** of these will result in failure

A driving fault : a less serious fault, but an accumulation of these may result in failure

Total driving faults :-

A serious fault : committing **one** of these will result in failure

The total number of driving faults made in all areas during the test

Your provisional driving licence

You must be at least 17 years of age before you can obtain a provisional car licence. However, as an exception, if you receive Disability Living Allowance at the higher rate you can obtain your provisional licence when you're 16.

You must hold a valid, signed provisional driving licence before you attempt to drive on the road.

Driving licences are issued by the Driver and Vehicle Licensing Agency (DVLA) but application form D1 can be obtained from any Post Office. In Northern Ireland the issuing authority is Driver and Vehicle Licensing Northern Ireland and the form is a DL1.

These forms need to be sent to the appropriate office, detailed on the form. You must enclose the required passport-type photographs as all provisional licences now issued are photocard licences.

When you receive your provisional licence, check that all details are correct. You must then sign it as it isn't valid until you do.

If you need to contact DVLA, telephone numbers are shown on page 77.

Vehicle insurance

The vehicle you practise in must be properly insured for you to drive. You will be asked to sign a declaration before the test begins.

If you drive while uninsured you will be committing a serious offence.

Don't risk it.

Approved Driving Instructor (ADI)

An ADI is approved by DSA to teach learner drivers for payment.

DSA is responsible for maintaining and checking the standards of all ADIs, who must

*   have held a full driving licence for at least four years
*   pass a written exam lasting 90 minutes
*   pass a strict driving test
*   reach and keep up a high standard of instruction. ADIs are regularly checked by a supervising examiner from DSA
*   be registered with DSA
*   display an ADI identification certificate on the windscreen of the tuition vehicle.

You must use an ADI or a trainee-licence holder if you want to pay someone to teach you the practical skills of driving. It is unlikely that anyone except an ADI would have the experience, knowledge and training to teach you properly.

Some trainee driving instructors are granted a trainee licence so that they can gain teaching experience before their qualifying examination. This licence is a pink identification certificate which must be displayed on the windscreen of the tuition vehicle.

Take advice from your ADI on

- all aspects of driving
- what books to read
- when you will be ready for your test
- how to practise
- further training after you have passed your test (Pass Plus scheme; see page 66).

How to choose an ADI

- Ask friends and relatives.
- Choose an instructor
  - who has a good reputation
  - is reliable and punctual
  - whose car suits you.

Voluntary Code of Practice

A voluntary Code of Practice has been agreed with the driving instruction industry. The code covers the following matters in relation to ADIs

- their level of qualification
- the personal conduct expected from them when giving tuition
- the professional conduct of their business
- the acceptability of their advertising
- their method of dealing with complaints.

For further information or advice telephone DSA HQ 0115 901 2500.

Study The Highway Code

- Know and understand *The Highway Code.*
- Obey it when driving.

Practising

If you are taking lessons with an ADI it's a good idea to take extra practice with a friend or relative. Ask your ADI for advice on this.

You must have with you a person who

- has held a full EC/EEA driving licence for at least three years and still holds one for the category of vehicle being driven
- is at least 21 years of age.

Where to practise

Practise

- on as many different types of road as you can
- in all sorts of traffic conditions – even in the dark
- on dual carriageways where the upper speed limit applies.

You may be asked to drive on such roads during the test. Don't just concentrate on exercises included in the test.

When you practise try not to

- obstruct other traffic. Most drivers are tolerant of learners, but don't try their patience too much
- annoy local residents. For example, don't repeatedly practise emergency stops in the same quiet residential streets or practise on test routes.

There are more helpful suggestions for the person accompanying you in the DSA book *The Official Guide to Accompanying L-Drivers.*

Am I ready for the test?

You will be ready for the test when you show that you have reached the standards set in this book – not before.

You should ensure that all of the aspects of the official syllabus have been covered (see Part Five).

The learners who pass first time do so because they are well instructed and get plenty of practice.

They pass because they **wait until they are ready.**

Your instructor has the knowledge and experience to tell you when you are ready.

If you and your instructor fill in your log book (as explained on page 11) it will help to indicate when you are ready.

You must be able to drive

- consistently well and with confidence
- without assistance and guidance from your instructor.

If you can't, you aren't ready for the test. Waiting until you are ready will save you time and money.

Completing a log book

This will help you monitor your progress, both during formal lessons and private practice.

Log books are available either from your ADI or from your local Driving Test Centre.

It is a voluntary scheme but the use of a log book will enable you to keep a record of your progress and provide you with a lasting record of your achievement.

It is a pocket-sized book, the main elements being

- **lesson record** – a record of your lessons

- **topic record** – a record of all topics covered in the recommended syllabus for learning to drive (see Part Five), with space for your instructor to fill in your progress. From this you will be able to see at a glance which topics you need to improve

- **private practice record** – space for you to keep a record of any driving you have done between lessons and any worries you have, so that you can discuss them with your instructor

- **theory test** – a tick list of topics covered in the theory test, to be completed by you and your instructor, again a quick reference as to your progress.

The test application form

You can obtain an application form (DL26) at any DSA driving test centre. Your ADI will also be able to give you a copy and tell you the fee to send with it.

Full details of all fees can be obtained from your nearest driving test centre or the DSA Enquiries and Booking Centre, telephone 0870 01 01 372.

Complete the form and send it to the address shown on the back.

At test centres in Wales, you can take a test in the Welsh language. Please indicate your choice on the test application form.

- Apply well before the time you want to be tested.
- Give your preferred date.

Booking by credit or debit card

You must be the card-holder. Visa, Mastercard, Switch and Delta are all accepted.

The telephone number to call is 0870 01 01 372.

If you use this service the driving test booking clerk will be able to offer you an appointment over the telephone. You should receive written notification confirming the appointment within a few days.

The booking clerk will want to know the following details

- your theory test pass certificate number, where applicable
- your driver number, shown on your licence

- the type of test you wish to book
- your personal details (name, address, day/evening telephone numbers)
- driving school code number (if known)
- your preferred date
- unacceptable days or periods
- if you can accept a test at short notice (consult your ADI beforehand, if necessary)
- disability or any special circumstances
- your credit/debit card number and its expiry date (and issue number, when using Switch).

Saturday and evening tests

Saturday and weekday evening tests are available at some driving test centres. The fees for these are higher than for a driving test during normal working hours on weekdays. Evening tests are available during the summer months only.

You can get details from

- DSA
- driving test centres
- your ADI.

Driving test fees

You may pay by

- cheque
- postal order
- credit/debit card.

Don't send cash.

Disabilities or special circumstances

To make sure that enough time is allowed for your test, it would help DSA to know if you

- are deaf or have severe hearing difficulties
- are in any way restricted in your movements
- have any disability which may affect your driving.

If any of these apply to you, please say so on your application form.

If you can't speak English or are deaf, you are allowed to bring an interpreter (who must not be an instructor). The interpreter must be 16 years or over.

No matter how serious your disability might be, you will still take the same driving test as every other test candidate. However, more time is allowed for the test. This is simply so that your examiner can talk to you about your disability and any adaptations fitted to your vehicle. If you would like further information, please see the list of useful addresses at the back of this book.

Your test appointment

DSA will send you notification of your appointment, which is the receipt for your fee. Take it with you when you go for your test.

It will include

- the time and place of your test
- the address of the driving test centre
- other important information.

If you haven't received notification after two weeks, contact DSA Enquiries and Booking Centre (0870 01 01 372).

Postponing your test appointment

Contact DSA if

- the date or time of the appointment isn't suitable
- you want to postpone or cancel your test.

You must give at least **ten clear working days'** notice (that is, two weeks – longer if there is a bank holiday), **not** counting

- the day DSA received your request
- the day of the test.

If you don't give enough notice you will lose your fee.

Documents

Make sure that you have your provisional driving licence **and** your theory test pass certificate with you when you arrive for your test. Check that you have signed your licence. Any of the following licences are acceptable

- a provisional driving licence issued in Great Britain (GB), or a GB full licence giving the provisional entitlement

- a provisional licence issued in Northern Ireland (NI), or a full licence giving the provisional entitlement

- an EC/EEA licence accompanied by a GB licence counterpart, if you want to take a test for a category not covered by your full EU licence.

If you have a full driving licence which was issued in another country but isn't eligible for exchange for a GB licence, you must apply for, and bring with you, a GB provisional licence. For information see DVLA information sheet D100, which is available from post offices.

Your examiner will not be able to conduct the test if you can't produce one of these licences.

If you have a photo licence you must bring with you the counterpart, which is part of the licence.

All documents must be original – DSA can't accept photocopies.

Photo identity

If your licence does not show your photograph you must also bring with you a form of photographic identification. For this your examiner will accept

- your passport, or document of like nature. Your passport doesn't have to be a British passport

- any of the following identification cards, provided it has your photograph and your signature
  - workplace identity card
  - trade union or students' union membership card
  - card for the purchase of reduced price rail tickets
  - school bus pass
  - cheque guarantee card or credit card
  - gun licence
  - proof of age card (issued by the Portman Group)

- a photograph of yourself, which has been signed and dated on the back by an acceptable person, confirming that the photograph is a true likeness of you. A signature will be accepted from the following
  - Approved Driving Instructor
  - DSA certified motorcycle instructor
  - Member of Parliament
  - local authority councillor
  - teacher (qualified)
  - Justice of the Peace
  - civil servant (established)
  - police officer
  - bank official
  - minister of religion
  - barrister or solicitor
  - medical practitioner
  - LGV trainer on DSA Voluntary Register of LGV Instructors
  - commissioned officer in HM forces.

Your test will be cancelled if you can't provide one of these forms of identification.

Your test vehicle

Make sure that the vehicle you intend to drive during the test is

- legally roadworthy and has a current MOT test certificate, if it's over the prescribed age
- fully covered by insurance for its present use and for you to drive.

Your examiner will ask you to sign a declaration that your insurance is in order. The test won't be conducted if you are unable to do so.

Note. A hire car is unlikely to be insured for the driving test. You should check with the hire company before you sign the declaration at the test centre.

Your vehicle should also display

- a valid tax disc (unless exempt)
- L-plates (or, if you wish, D-plates, if taking your test in Wales) displayed to the front and rear

The plates shouldn't be displayed on the windscreen or back window. Both you and your examiner should have a clear view of the road.

Your vehicle must also have

- a fully functional seat belt fitted to the front passenger seat
- a head restraint fitted to the front passenger seat ('slip-on' type head restraints are not permissible on test)
- an additional interior rear-view mirror suitable for use by the examiner.

Specially adapted vehicles may be exempt from these requirements.

If you overlook any of these

- your test will be cancelled
- you will lose your fee.

The condition of your vehicle

Your vehicle must be mechanically sound. All equipment required by law must be fitted and working correctly.

Many modern vehicles are equipped with a spare wheel intended for temporary use. Your vehicle won't be suitable to use for the test if one of these spare wheels is in use.

The controls, seating, equipment or any other articles in the vehicle must be arranged so that they don't interfere with the conduct of the test.

A dual accelerator (if fitted) must be removed before the test.

I .... (name of certifier), certify that this is a true likeness of .... , who has been known to me for (number) months / years in my capacity as ....

Signed

Dated

15

Seat belts

If the law requires your vehicle to have seat belts, make sure that they

- work properly
- are clean and in a satisfactory condition.

Wear your seat belt, unless you have a medical exemption certificate.

You are allowed to remove your seat belt to carry out a manoeuvre which involves reversing. Make sure that you refasten it immediately afterwards.

Head restraints

Most modern vehicles are fitted with head restraints to provide protection in the event of an accident or heavy braking. If your vehicle has them fitted, please don't remove them before coming for your test.

Left-hand drive vehicles

If you are driving a left-hand drive vehicle, take special care and make full use of your mirrors.

Unsuitable vehicles for a car driving test

- Vehicles with no clear view to the rear – other than by use of the exterior mirrors.
- Vehicles with only a driver's seat.
- Vehicles with more than eight passenger seats.
- Loaded or partly loaded vehicles.
- Vehicles over 3.5 tonnes in weight.
- Vehicles towing trailers (For vehicles towing trailers see Part Three).

You will lose your fee if the vehicle isn't suitable for the test.

Bribery

It is a criminal offence to attempt to bribe an examiner in any way.

When you have passed

You will be allowed to drive

- without L- or D-plates (if you are driving in Wales you are permitted to use D-plates instead of L-plates)
- unsupervised
- on motorways.

It takes lots of practice to become a skilled driver. Further tuition and the Pass Plus scheme (see page 66) are strongly recommended.

Part Two

The driving test

This part looks at what the test requires.

The topics covered

- The eyesight test
- Theory into practice
- Before you start the engine
- The car controls
- Other controls
- Moving off
- Using the mirrors
- Giving signals
- Acting on signs and signals
- Controlling your speed
- Making progress
- The emergency stop
- Reversing around a corner
- Reverse parking
- Turning in the road
- Hazards
- Selecting a safe place to stop
- Awareness and anticipation.

What the test requires

You must satisfy your examiner that, in good daylight, you can read a vehicle number plate with letters 79.4 mm (3.1 in.) high at a **minimum distance** of 20.5 metres (about 67 feet). Number plates with a narrower font, such as the new style number plates introduced during 2001, should be read from a distance of 20 metres (66 feet).

If you need glasses or contact lenses to read the number plate, that is fine. However, you must wear them during the test and whenever you drive.

If you have had sight correction surgery you should declare this when you apply for your provisional licence.

How your examiner will test you

Before you get into your car your examiner will point out a vehicle and ask you to read its number plate.

If you can't speak English or have difficulty reading, you may copy down what you see.

If your answer is incorrect, your examiner will measure the exact distance and repeat the test.

If you fail the eyesight test

If you can't show your examiner that your eyesight is up to the required standard

- you will have failed your driving test
- your test will go no further.

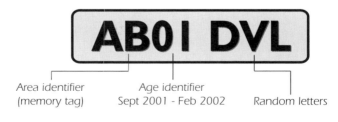

If you normally wear glasses or contact lenses, always wear them whenever you drive.

ABOI DVL

Area identifier   Age identifier
(memory tag)   Sept 2001 - Feb 2002   Random letters

What the test requires

You must satisfy your examiner that you have **fully understood** everything which you learned for the theory test.

The aspects are

- alertness and concentration
- courtesy and consideration
- care in the use of the controls to reduce mechanical wear and tear
- awareness of stopping distances and safety margins in all conditions
- hazard awareness
- correct action concerning pedestrians and other vulnerable road users
- dealing with other types of vehicle in the correct manner
- rules regarding speed limits and stopping restrictions
- road and traffic signs.

You will also be expected to know

- the law regarding you and your vehicle
- what to do in the event of an accident
- the effect extra loads have on your vehicle
- the effect motoring has on the environment.

How your examiner will test you

Your examiner will give you a few moments to get settled into your vehicle. She or he will then ask you to go ahead, unless you are asked to turn or the traffic signs direct you otherwise.

Throughout the test your examiner will expect you to demonstrate the knowledge you have gained by studying for your theory test.

What your examiner wants to see

Before you start the engine you must always check that

- all doors are properly closed
- your seat is properly adjusted
- the head restraints are fitted and properly adjusted
- your driving mirrors are properly adjusted
- your seat belt is fastened, correctly adjusted and comfortable, with both the lap belt and the diagonal belt protecting your body
- the handbrake is on
- the gear lever is in neutral or, if you are driving an automatic vehicle, the gear lever is in P (park) or N (neutral).

Develop this routine while you are learning.

Faults to avoid

You shouldn't

- leave these checks until after you have started the engine
- attempt to adjust the mirrors or the seat position while the car is moving. This could be dangerous.

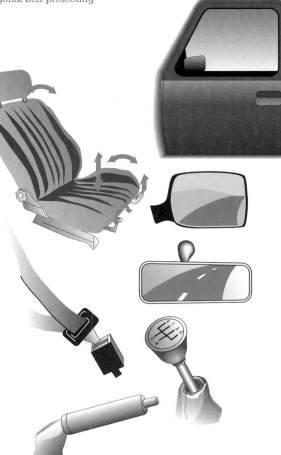

What the test requires

You should show your examiner that you understand the functions of all the controls.

You should use them

- smoothly
- correctly
- safely
- at the right time.

The main controls are

- accelerator
- clutch
- footbrake
- handbrake (this may sometimes be referred to as the parking brake)
- steering
- gears.

You should

- understand what these controls do
- be able to use them competently.

If you are driving an automatic vehicle

Make sure that you fully understand the procedure required before you attempt to drive a vehicle with automatic transmission.

Accelerator and clutch

Skills you should show

You should

- balance the accelerator and clutch to pull away smoothly
- accelerate gradually to gain speed
- press the clutch in just before the car stops.

If you are driving an automatic vehicle, you should

- ensure that your foot is on the footbrake when you engage 'drive' (D)
- use the accelerator gradually to
  - avoid the vehicle surging forward (or backward) out of control
  - control the upward gear changes.

Faults to avoid

You shouldn't

- accelerate fiercely, especially making the tyres screech. This can lead to a loss of control and may distract or alarm other road users
- use the clutch in a jerky and uncontrolled manner when moving off or changing gear.

If you are driving an automatic vehicle, you shouldn't cause the vehicle to surge by harsh use of the accelerator.

Footbrake, handbrake and gears

Skills you should show

Footbrake

You should brake

- smoothly and in good time
- lightly in most situations.

Handbrake

You should

- know how and when to apply the handbrake.

Gears

You should

- choose the right gear for your speed and the road conditions
- change gear in good time so that you are ready for a hazard or junction.

If you are driving an automatic vehicle, select a low gear if you are going down a steep hill.

Faults to avoid

Footbrake

You shouldn't

- brake harshly, except in an emergency.

Handbrake

You shouldn't

- apply the handbrake before the car has stopped
- move off with the handbrake on.

Gears

You shouldn't

- take your eyes off the road to look at the gear lever
- coast with the clutch pedal depressed or the gear lever in neutral.

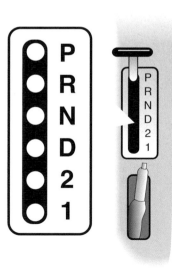

Steering

Skills you should show

You should

- place your hands on the steering wheel in either the 'ten-to-two' or 'quarter-to-three' position, whichever is more comfortable
- keep your steering movements steady and smooth
- begin turning the wheel at the correct time when turning a corner.

Faults to avoid

Don't turn too early when steering around a corner. If you do, you risk

- cutting the corner when turning right and putting other drivers at risk
- striking the kerb when turning left.

Don't turn too late. You could put other road users at risk by

- swinging wide on left turns
- overshooting right turns.

You shouldn't

- cross your hands on the steering wheel
- allow the wheel to spin back after turning
- rest your arm on the door.

Correct hand positions for driving

What the test requires

You should understand

- the functions of all controls and switches which have a bearing on road safety
  - indicators
  - lights
  - windscreen wipers
  - demisters
  - heater.

You should know where to find these controls on the vehicle you are driving

- the meaning of gauges or other displays on the instrument panel
  - speedometer
  - various warning lights.

Safety checks

You should also be able to carry out routine safety checks such as

- oil and coolant levels
- tyre pressures.

In addition, you should be able to identify defects, especially with

- steering
- brakes
- tyres
- seat belts
- lights
- reflectors
- horn
- rear view mirrors
- speedometer
- exhaust system
- direction indicators
- windscreen wipers and washers.

You should understand the effects which extra loads have on your vehicle. Loads such as

- a roof rack and luggage
- extra passengers.

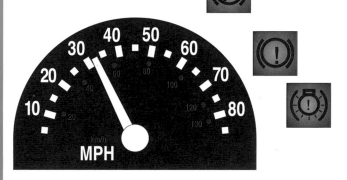

What the test requires

You should be able to move off

- safely
- under control
- on the flat
- from behind a parked car
- on a hill, where appropriate.

How your examiner will test you

Your examiner will watch your

- use of the controls each time you move off
- observation of other road users.

Skills you should show

Use your mirrors and signal if necessary.

Before you move off, look around over your shoulder and check any blind spots that can't be seen in your mirror. Check for

- traffic
- pedestrians.

Move off under control making balanced use of the

- accelerator
- clutch
- brakes
- steering.

You should also ensure that you move off in the correct gear.

Faults to avoid

You shouldn't

- immediately signal without first taking effective observation around you
- pull out without looking
- cause other road users to stop or alter their course
- accelerate excessively
- move off in too high a gear
- fail to co-ordinate the controls correctly and stall the engine.

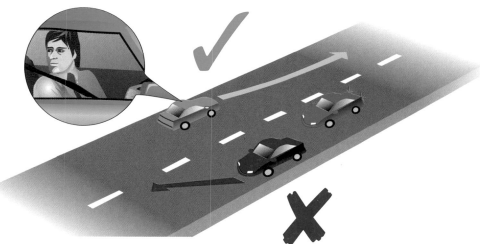

USING THE MIRRORS

What the test requires

Make sure that you use your mirrors effectively

- before any manoeuvre
- to keep aware of what is happening behind you.

Check carefully before

- moving off
- signalling
- changing direction
- turning to the left or right
- overtaking or changing lanes
- increasing speed
- slowing down or stopping
- opening your car door.

How your examiner will test you

For this aspect of driving there is no special test. Your examiner will watch your use of mirrors as you drive.

Skills you should show

Use the Mirrors – Signal – Manoeuvre (MSM) routine. This is fully explained on page 38.

You should

- look before you signal
- look and signal before you act
- act sensibly and safely on what you see in the mirrors.

You should be aware that the mirrors won't show everything behind you.

Faults to avoid

You shouldn't

- manoeuvre without looking in the mirrors
- fail to act on what you see when you look in the mirrors.

Act on what you see. Just looking isn't enough.

28

What the test requires

You should signal

- to let others know what you intend to do
- to help other road users, including pedestrians
- in plenty of time.

You must only use the signals shown in *The Highway Code*.

Your signals should help other road users

- to understand what you intend to do
- to react safely.

Always make sure that your signal is cancelled after use.

How your examiner will test you

For this aspect of the driving test there is no special exercise. Your examiner will watch carefully how you use your signals as you drive.

Skills you should show

Give signals

- clearly
- in good time.

You should also know how to give arm signals and when they are necessary.

Faults to avoid

You shouldn't

- give signals carelessly
- mislead other road users
- forget to cancel the signal
- wave at pedestrians to cross the road.

What the test requires

You should be able to understand

- all traffic signs
- all road markings.

React to them in good time.

At the beginning of the test your examiner will ask you to follow the road ahead.

You will be **asked** to turn at junctions, but look out for lane markings and direction signs. You will be expected to act on these.

Traffic lights

You must act correctly at traffic lights.

When the green light shows, check that the road is clear before proceeding.

Signals by authorised persons

You must obey the signals given by

- police officers
- traffic wardens
- school crossing patrols.

Traffic calming measures

Take extra care on roads which have been altered by the addition of

- 20 mph speed limit zones
- speed restriction humps
- width restrictions marked by bollards, posts or paved areas.

What the test requires

You should make good progress along the road bearing in mind

- road conditions
- traffic
- weather
- road signs and speed limits.

How your examiner will test you

For this aspect of driving there is no special exercise. Your examiner will watch carefully your control of speed as you drive.

Skills you should show

You should

- take great care in the use of speed
- make sure that you can stop safely, well within the distance you can see to be clear
- leave a safe distance between yourself and other vehicles
- leave extra distance on wet or slippery roads
- approach junctions and hazards at the correct speed.

Faults to avoid

You shouldn't

- drive too fast for the road and traffic conditions
- change your speed unpredictably.

What the test requires

You should

- make reasonable progress along the road
- drive at a speed appropriate to road and traffic conditions
- move off at junctions as soon as it is safe to do so.

How your examiner will test you

For this aspect of driving there is no special exercise. Your examiner will watch your driving and will want to see you

- make reasonable progress along the road
- keep up with traffic
- show confidence, together with sound judgement
- comply with the speed limits.

Skills you should show

You should be able to choose the correct speed for the

- type of road
- type and density of traffic
- weather and visibility.

You should approach all hazards at a safe speed.

Faults to avoid

You shouldn't

- drive too slowly, holding up other traffic
- be over-cautious or stop and wait when it's safe to go
- prepare too early for junctions by approaching too slowly and holding up traffic.

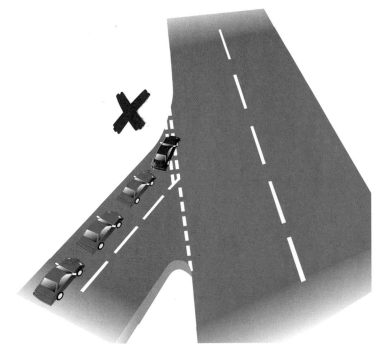

What the test requires

In an emergency you should be able to stop the car

- as quickly as possible
- safely and under control
- without locking the wheels.

How your examiner will test you

Your examiner may

- ask you to pull up on the side of the road
- ask you to make an emergency stop when you are given the signal
- demonstrate the signal to you.

When your examiner gives the signal, try to stop the car as you would in a real emergency.

- You should react quickly.
- Try to stop in a straight line.
- Take special care if the road is wet.

Your examiner will check that the road is clear behind you before the signal is given.

Skills you should show

You should stop the car

- in a short distance
- under full control
- without risk to other road users.

Faults to avoid

You shouldn't

- anticipate the signal by stopping while your examiner is checking the road behind
- skid out of control
- allow the car to swing off course.

What the test requires

You should be able to reverse your car

- smoothly
- correctly
- safely
- under full control.

How your examiner will test you

Your examiner will normally

- ask you to pull up just before a side road on the left
- point out the side road and ask you to reverse into it.

You may undo your seat belt for the whole of the exercise. Do so only if it interferes with your driving. Don't forget to refasten it after you have completed the exercise.

If the view to the rear is restricted (in a van, for example) your examiner might ask you to reverse into a road on the right.

When your examiner asks you, you should

- make sure that you can carry out the exercise correctly and safely
- check traffic and road conditions in all directions
- reverse around the corner keeping a good lookout for traffic or pedestrians
- straighten up your car and continue to reverse for a reasonable distance
- pull up in a safe position and wait for your examiner's next instruction.

Your car will swing out at the front as you reverse around the corner. Keep a good lookout for other road users.

Skills you should show

You should

- reverse under full control
- keep reasonably close to the kerb, without striking or mounting it
- use good, effective all-round observation.

Faults to avoid

You shouldn't

- mount the kerb
- swing out wide
- reverse too far from the kerb
- be inconsiderate to other road users
- take more than a reasonable time to complete the exercise, creating a hazard for other road users
- steer harshly while the car is stationary (dry steering).

What the test requires

You should be able to park your car safely either at the kerb (by reversing into the space of about two car lengths) or off the road (by reversing neatly into a bay).

How your examiner will test you

Parking at the kerb behind a parked car

After your examiner has explained what is required you should

- drive alongside the parked vehicle and position your car so that you can carry out the exercise correctly and safely

- select reverse gear – your reversing lights might help others to understand your intentions

- use effective all-round observation

- reverse into the space behind the parked car, within the space of about two car lengths

- stop reasonably close, and parallel, to the kerb.

Keep a good lookout for traffic and pedestrians all the time.

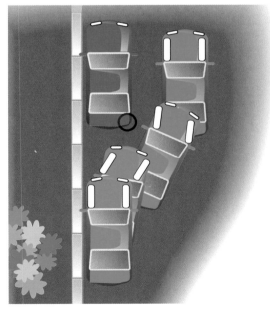

Reversing into a parking bay

You should

- look at the layout markings and the size of the space available
- use your mirrors and signal if necessary
- check your position and keep your speed down
- use effective all-round observation
- look out for pedestrians
- reverse and park as neatly as possible, with your wheels straight
- make sure that your vehicle is neatly parked between the layout markings in the bay.

Skills you should show

You should

- reverse under full control, safely and steadily
- use good, effective all-round observation
- show consideration to other road users.

Faults to avoid

You shouldn't

- get too close to a parked car or the layout markings
- mount the kerb
- swing your car from side to side
- park, at an angle, too far from the kerb or layout markings
- place too much reliance on interior/exterior mirrors rather than taking good effective all-round observation
- be inconsiderate or cause a danger to other road users
- take more than a reasonable time to complete the exercise. This may cause an obstruction for other road users
- steer harshly while the vehicle is stationary (dry steering).

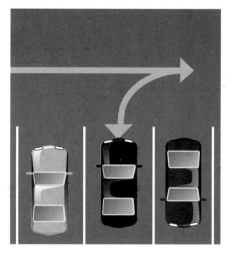

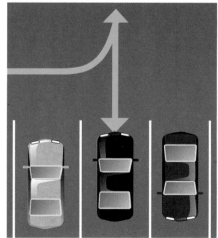

What the test requires

You should be able to turn your car around in the road

- so that it faces in the opposite direction
- using the forward and reverse gears.

This will take at least three moves.

How your examiner will test you

Your examiner will

- indicate a suitable place and ask you to pull up
- ask you to turn your car around in the road.

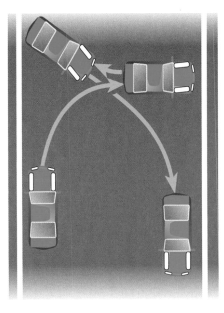

You should

- make sure that the road is clear in both directions
- drive forward in first gear, turning the steering wheel to the right as much as possible
- steer briskly to the left just before you pull up close to the opposite kerb
- check all around, especially your blind spots
- reverse, turning your steering wheel to the left as much as possible
- steer briskly to the right before you pull up close to the kerb behind you
- repeat if necessary until your car is facing in the opposite direction.

Skills you should show

You should control your car smoothly. Make proper use of the

- accelerator
- clutch
- brakes
- steering.

Show awareness of other road users. All-round observation is essential throughout the manoeuvre.

Faults to avoid

You shouldn't

- mount the kerb (try not to touch it)
- be inconsiderate or cause danger to other road users
- take more than a reasonable time to complete the exercise, causing an obstruction for other road users
- steer harshly while the car is stationary (dry steering).

What is a hazard?

A hazard is any situation which could involve adjusting speed or altering course.

Look well ahead where there are

- road junctions or roundabouts
- parked vehicles
- cyclists or horse riders
- pedestrian crossings.

By identifying the hazard early you will have time to take the appropriate action.

You may have to deal with several hazards at once or during a short space of time. This may mean using your initiative and common sense to deal with the particular circumstances.

What the test requires

Mirrors – Signal –Manoeuvre (MSM routine)

Always use this routine when approaching a hazard.

M – Mirrors

Check the position of traffic around and behind you.

S – Signal

Signal your intention to change course or slow down. Signal in good time.

M – Manoeuvre

A manoeuvre is any change of speed or position, from slowing or stopping the car to turning off a busy road.

What the test requires

You should

- use the MSM routine when you approach a junction or a roundabout
- position your car correctly. Adjust your speed and stop if necessary
- use the correct lane if the road has lane markings. In a one-way street choose that lane as soon as you can do so safely.

If the road has no lane markings, when turning left, keep to the left.

Watch out for

- motorcyclists
- cyclists
- pedestrians crossing.

When turning right, you should

- keep as close to the centre of the road as is safe
- use effective observation before you enter a junction.

How your examiner will test you

For this aspect of driving there is no special exercise. Your examiner will watch carefully and take account of your

- use of the MSM routine
- position and speed on approach
- observation and judgement.

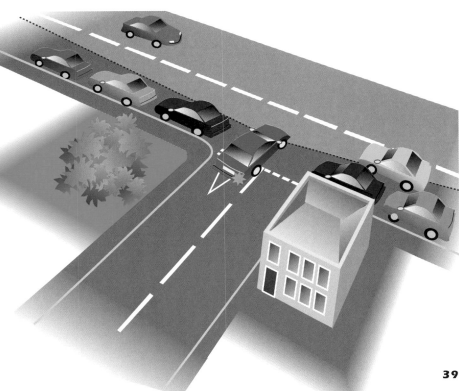

Skills you should show

You should be able to

- observe road signs and markings and act correctly on what you see
- judge the correct speed on approach
- slow down in good time, without harsh braking
- judge the speed of the other traffic, especially at roundabouts and when you are joining major roads
- position and turn correctly.

Faults to avoid

You shouldn't

- approach the junction at the wrong speed
- position and turn incorrectly
- enter a junction unsafely
- stop or wait unnecessarily.

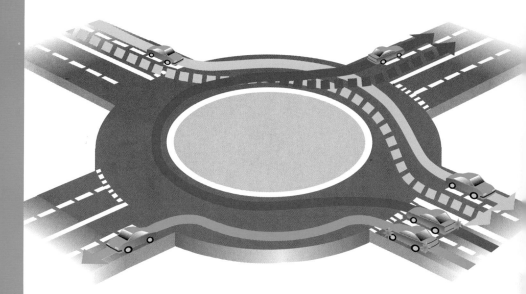

What the test requires

When overtaking you must

- observe any signs and road markings which prohibit overtaking
- allow enough room
- give motorcyclists, cyclists and horses at least as much room as a car. They might swerve or wobble suddenly
- allow enough space after overtaking. Don't cut in.

How your examiner will test you

For this aspect of driving there is no special exercise. Your examiner will watch and take into account how you

- use the MSM routine
- react to road and traffic conditions
- handle the controls.

Skills you should show

You should be able to judge the speed and position of vehicles

- behind, which might be trying to overtake you
- in front, if you are planning to overtake
- coming towards you.

Overtake only when you can do so

- safely
- without causing other vehicles to slow down or alter course.

Faults to avoid

You shouldn't overtake when

- your view of the road ahead isn't clear
- you would have to exceed the speed limit
- the road is narrow.

What the test requires

You should deal with oncoming traffic safely and confidently. This applies

- on narrow roads
- where there are parked cars or other obstructions.

If there is an obstruction on your side of the road, or not enough space for two vehicles to pass safely, you should

- use the MSM routine
- be prepared to give way to oncoming traffic.

If you need to stop, keep well back from the obstruction to give yourself

- a better view of the road ahead
- room to move off easily when the road is clear.

When you are passing parked cars, allow at least the width of a car door, if possible.

How your examiner will test you

For this aspect of driving there is no special exercise. Your examiner will watch carefully and take into account how you

- use the MSM routine
- react to road and traffic conditions
- handle the controls.

Skills you should show

You should

- show judgement and control when meeting oncoming traffic
- be decisive when stopping and moving off
- allow enough room when passing parked cars.

Watch out for

- doors opening
- children running out into the road
- pedestrians stepping out from the pavement
- vehicles pulling out without warning.

What the test requires

You should be able to cross the path of other vehicles safely and with confidence.

You normally need to cross the path of other vehicles when you have to turn right into a side road or driveway. You should

- use the MSM routine
- position your car correctly and adjust your speed
- keep as close to the centre of the road as is safe
- watch out for oncoming traffic and stop if necessary.

Watch out for pedestrians

- crossing the side road
- on the pavement, if you are entering a driveway.

If you stop behind another vehicle in a queue of traffic, leave enough room to pull out if the car in front breaks down.

How your examiner will test you

For this aspect of driving there is no special exercise. Your examiner will watch carefully and take account of your judgement of the oncoming traffic.

Skills you should show

You should show that you can turn right into a junction or driveway safely, using the MSM routine.

Faults to avoid

You shouldn't cause other vehicles to

- slow down
- swerve
- stop.

You shouldn't

- cut the corner
- go beyond the correct turning point before you begin to turn.

What the test requires

You should always drive so that you can stop in the distance you can see to be clear.

Always keep a safe distance between yourself and the vehicle in front.

In good conditions, leave a gap of at least one metre (just over three feet) for every mile per hour you are travelling. Or leave a two-second time gap.

In bad conditions, leave at least double the distance, or a four-second time gap.

In slow-moving, congested traffic it may not be practical to leave so much space.

How your examiner will test you

For this aspect of driving there is no special exercise. Your examiner will watch carefully and take account of how you

* use the MSM routine
* anticipate situations
* react to changing road and traffic conditions
* handle the controls.

Skills you should show

You should

* be able to judge a safe separation distance between you and the vehicle in front
* show correct use of the MSM routine, especially before reducing speed
* avoid the need to brake harshly if the vehicle in front slows down or stops
* take extra care when your view ahead is limited by large vehicles such as lorries or buses.

Watch out for

* brake lights ahead
* direction indicators
* vehicles ahead braking without warning.

Faults to avoid

You shouldn't

* follow too closely
* brake suddenly
* stop too close to the vehicle in front in a traffic queue.

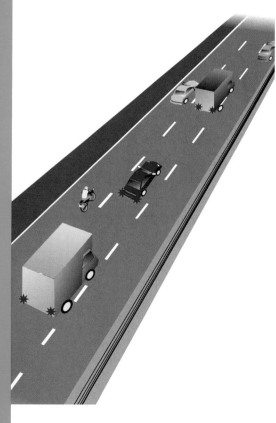

What the test requires

You should

- normally keep well to the left
- keep clear of parked vehicles
- avoid weaving in and out between parked vehicles
- position your vehicle correctly for the direction you intend to take.

You should obey all lane markings, especially

- bus and cycle lanes
- in one-way streets

and be particularly aware of left- or right-turn arrows at junctions.

How your examiner will test you

For this aspect of driving there is no special exercise. Your examiner will watch carefully to see that you

- use the MSM routine
- select the correct lane in good time.

Skills you should show

You should

- plan ahead and choose the correct lane in good time
- use the MSM routine correctly
- position your vehicle sensibly, even if there are no road markings.

Faults to avoid

You shouldn't

- drive too close to the kerb
- drive too close to the centre of the road
- change lanes at the last moment or without good reason
- hinder other road users by being badly positioned or being in the wrong lane
- straddle lanes or lane markings
- cut across the path of other traffic in another lane at roundabouts.

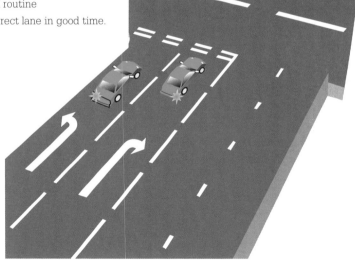

What the test requires

You should

- recognise the different types of pedestrian crossing
- show courtesy and consideration towards pedestrians
- stop safely when necessary.

At zebra crossings

You must slow down and stop if there is anyone on the crossing.

You should also

- slow down and be prepared to stop if there is anyone waiting to cross
- know how to give the correct arm signal, if necessary, before slowing down or stopping.

At pelican, puffin and toucan crossings

You must

- stop if the lights are red
- give way to any pedestrians on a pelican crossing when the amber lights are flashing
- give way to cyclists on a toucan crossing, as you would to pedestrians.

How your examiner will test you

For this aspect of driving there is no special exercise. Your examiner will watch carefully and take account of how you deal with pedestrian crossings.

Skills you should show

You should be able to

- approach a pedestrian crossing at a controlled speed
- stop safely when necessary
- move off when it's safe, keeping a good lookout.

Faults to avoid

Don't

- approach a crossing too fast
- drive over a crossing without stopping or showing awareness of waiting pedestrians
- block a crossing by stopping directly on it.

Don't hurry pedestrians by

- sounding your horn
- revving your engine
- edging forward.

Don't

- overtake within the zigzag white lines leading up to crossings
- wave pedestrians across
- take late or incorrect action on traffic light signals at controlled crossings.

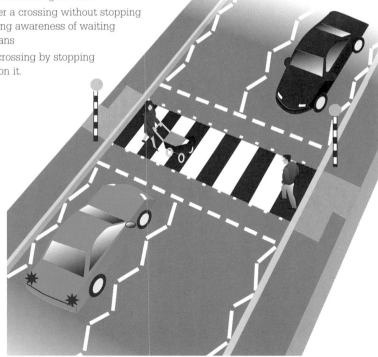

What the test requires

When you make a normal stop you should be able to select a place where you won't

- obstruct the road
- create a hazard.

You should stop close to the edge of the road.

How your examiner will test you

For this aspect of driving there is no special exercise. Your examiner will watch your driving and take account of your

- use of the MSM routine
- judgement in selecting a safe place to stop.

Skills you should show

You should know how and where to stop without causing inconvenience or danger to other road users.

Faults to avoid

You shouldn't

- stop without sufficient warning to other road users
- cause danger or inconvenience to other road users when you stop.

What the test requires

You should be aware of other road users at all times. Also, always plan ahead.

You should

- judge what other road users are going to do
- predict how their actions will affect you
- react safely and in good time.

Skills you should show

You should show awareness of, and consideration for, all other road users. Anticipation of possible danger and concern for safety should also be shown.

Pedestrians

You should

- give way to pedestrians when turning from one road to another
- take particular care with the very young, the disabled and the elderly. They may not have seen you and could step out suddenly.

Cyclists

Take special care

- when crossing bus or cycle lanes
- with cyclists passing on your left
- with child cyclists.

Moped riders and motorcyclists

Look out for moped riders and motorcyclists

- in slow-moving traffic
- coming up on your left
- at junctions.

Animals

Take special care around animals. Give horse riders and other animal handlers as much room as you can. Watch young, possibly inexperienced, riders closely for signs of any difficulty with their mounts. Plan your approach carefully.

Faults to avoid

You shouldn't

- react suddenly to road or traffic conditions
- show irritation with other road users
- sound the horn aggressively
- rev your engine or edge forward when waiting for pedestrians to cross a road.

Part Three

Towing a trailer

This part looks at what is required when towing a trailer.

The topics covered

- Before the test
- The reversing exercise
- The braking exercise
- The drive
- Uncoupling and recoupling.

Cars towing trailers or caravans

You must pass a category B theory and practical test before towing a trailer.

If you want to tow a large trailer and you don't hold a full driving licence issued before 1 January 1997, you may have to take a further test (category B + E).

The booklet INS 57, enclosed with your provisional licence, or DVLA factsheet INF 30 'Towing Trailers in Great Britain' will give you the full information.

When you practise

When you practise you must

- display L-plates (or if you wish, D-plates in Wales) front and rear. These must be clearly visible
- be accompanied by a person who has held, for three years, and still holds, a licence for category B + E . They must be 21 years old or over.

Where and what to practise

You should practise

- on as many different roads as you can
- in all sorts of traffic conditions.

Practise reversing your vehicle and trailer. You will be given a reversing exercise during your test. When you practise, try not to obstruct other traffic.

You should practise turning left and right, taking into consideration the extra length of the unit. Be aware of your trailer when taking sharp turns.

Practise uncoupling and recoupling your vehicle and trailer. You will be asked to demonstrate this at the end of your test.

Test syllabus

The officially recommended syllabus for learning to drive vehicles with trailers (category B + E) can be found on pages 73–5.

Further information and advice on towing trailers can be found in *The Driving Manual* (The Stationery Office).

The test will include an eyesight test. You must be able to read a number plate with letters 79.4 mm (3.1 in.) high from 20.5 metres (about 67 feet). Number plates with a narrower font, such as the new style number plates introduced during 2001, should be read from a distance of 20 metres (66 feet)

If you need glasses or contact lenses to read the number plate, you must wear them when you are driving.

Your driving licence

Make sure that you have your full licence with provisional B + E entitlement with you and that you have signed it. Any of the following licences are acceptable

- a licence issued in Great Britain (GB)
- a licence issued in Northern Ireland (NI).

Your examiner might not be able to conduct your test if you can't produce one of these documents.

Your test vehicle

Make sure that the vehicle you intend to drive during your test is

- legally roadworthy and has a current MOT test certificate if it's over three years old
- fully covered by insurance for its present use and for you to drive. Your examiner will ask you to sign a declaration that your insurance is in order. The test won't be conducted if you are unable to do so
- properly licensed with a valid tax disc displayed
- displaying L-plates (or if you wish, D-plates in Wales) to the front of your vehicle and the rear of your trailer. They shouldn't be displayed on the windscreen (both you and your examiner must have a clear view of the road).

Make sure that the trailer you intend to tow is

- legally roadworthy
- at least 1 tonne Maximum Authorised Mass (MAM).

If you overlook any of these

- your test will be cancelled
- you will lose your fee.

The size of the reversing area will be set out according to the size of your vehicle and trailer together, as a unit.

Cones A and A1 are positioned starting one metre (just over three feet) into the area from the boundary line.

Distance A to A1 is one-and-a-half times the width of the widest part of the unit.

A to B is twice the length of the vehicle and trailer.

The overall length of the manoeuvre will be five times the length of the vehicle and trailer.

The width of the bay will be one-and-a-half times the widest part of the unit.

The length of the bay will be based on the overall length of the vehicle and trailer as a unit. The bay can be varied at the discretion of your examiner, within the range of plus one metre (three feet) or minus two metres (six feet).

The precise length of the bay won't be disclosed before the start of the exercise.

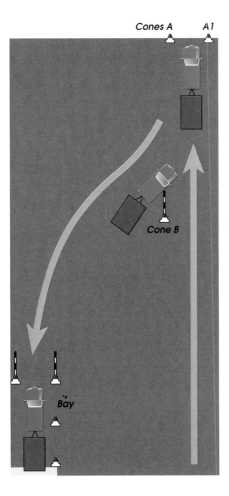

Cones A   A1

Cone B

Bay

What the test requires

You should be able to reverse your vehicle and trailer in a restricted space. You should be able to do this

- under control and in reasonable time
- with good observation
- with reasonable accuracy
- starting at a fixed point (cones A and A1)
- inside a clearly defined boundary
- by reversing so that you pass cone B on the offside of your vehicle
- so that the extreme rear of your trailer is within the painted yellow box area at the end of the bay when you stop.

Your examiner will show you a diagram of the manoeuvring area and explain what is required.

Skills you should show

You should complete the exercise

- reversing under full control
- using good, all-round observation
- ensuring accurate judgement of the size of your vehicle and trailer.

Faults to avoid

You shouldn't

- approach the starting point too fast
- approach cones A and A1 at an angle
- stop beyond the first marker cones A and A1
- turn the steering wheel incorrectly when starting to reverse
- over-steer so that any wheel goes over the yellow boundary
- fail to use effective observation around the vehicle
- allow any part of your vehicle to hit any of the cones or poles
- stop so that the rear of your vehicle and trailer is either short of or beyond the yellow box in the bay.

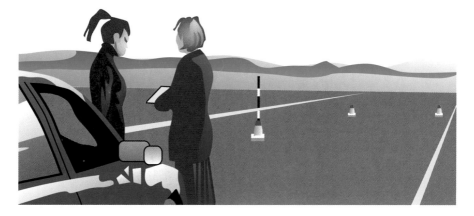

What the test requires

For safety reasons, the braking exercise will take place on a special manoeuvring area and not on the public roads.

Your examiner will be with you in the vehicle for this exercise.

She or he will point out two marker cones approximately 61 metres (200 feet) ahead. You should build up a speed of about 20 mph. When the front of the vehicle passes between the two markers you should apply the brakes. You should stop your vehicle and trailer with safety and under full control.

Skills you should show

You should stop the vehicle

- as quickly as possible
- under full control
- as safely as possible
- in a straight line.

Faults to avoid

You shouldn't

- drive too slowly (less than 20 mph)
- brake too soon (anticipate the marker points)
- brake too harshly, causing skidding
- depress the clutch too late (stalling the engine)
- take too long to stop.

Start

THE DRIVE

What the test requires

Your examiner will expect you to drive to a standard at least that of the driving test for category B.

The test will be approximately one hour long. It will include a wide variety of roads and traffic conditions.

The route will include roads carrying two-way traffic, dual carriageways and, where possible, one-way systems.

You will be expected to demonstrate that you can move off smoothly and safely both uphill and downhill. You will also have to move off normally from the side of the road and at an angle.

You **won't** be required to carry out the following exercises

- emergency stop on the road
- reversing around a corner
- reverse parking
- turning in the road.

Skills you should show

You will need to show that you can safely

- meet other vehicles
- overtake
- cross the path of other vehicles
- keep a safe separation distance
- negotiate various types of roundabout
- exercise correct lane discipline
- display courtesy and consideration to other road users especially
  - pedestrians
  - horseriders
  - cyclists
  - motorcyclists
- apply the correct procedure at
  - pedestrian crossings
  - level crossings
  - traffic signals
  - road junctions.

You will need to show

- effective use of the mirrors
- correct use of signals
- alertness and anticipation
- correct use of speed
- observation of speed limits
- care in the use of the controls to reduce mechanical wear and tear.

Fault to avoid

You shouldn't

- negotiate hazards and junctions dangerously through not using good, all-round observation.

What the test requires

When uncoupling you should

- ensure that the brakes are applied on both the vehicle and the trailer (extra care should be taken in the case of an ALCO chassis as the anti-reverse mechanism needs to be overcome)
- ensure that the jockey wheel is lowered correctly
- disconnect the electric line(s) and stow away safely
- remove any fitted stabilising equipment
- remove any safety chain or coupling
- release the coupling and move the trailer clear of the towing hook
- pull forward approximately one vehicle length.

When recoupling you should

- move the towing vehicle so that the trailer can be safely and easily coupled to it, and apply the parking brake
- attach the trailer to the towing vehicle and check that the coupling is secure by using a method appropriate to the vehicle and trailer
- attach any safety chain or device
- fit any necessary stabilising equipment
- connect the electric line(s)
- ensure that the wheels, legs or other supporting devices are raised and secured safely
- release the trailer brake, ensuring that the handbrake of the towing vehicle is firmly applied
- check the operation of the lights and indicators.

How your examiner will test you

You will normally be asked to uncouple and recouple your vehicle and trailer at the test centre at the end of the test.

Your examiner will ask you to

- stop where there is safe and level ground
- demonstrate the uncoupling of your vehicle and trailer
- pull forward approximately one vehicle length
- reverse the vehicle up to the trailer
- recouple the vehicle and trailer.

Your examiner will expect you to make sure that the

- coupling is secure
- lights and indicators are operating
- trailer brake is released.

If you have a disability which makes it difficult to complete this exercise, please state this when you book your test.

Skills you should show

You should be able to uncouple and recouple your vehicle and trailer

- in the correct sequence
- confidently and without any unnecessary delay.

Faults to avoid

When uncoupling

You shouldn't

- start the uncoupling without applying the brakes on both the vehicle and the trailer
- release the trailer coupling without the wheels or legs lowered
- move forward before the entire correct procedure has been completed.

When recoupling

You shouldn't

- fail to check that the brakes are applied on the trailer
- fail to use good, effective observation
- recouple at speed.

Don't attempt to move away without

- raising the wheels or legs
- checking
  - lights
  - indicators
  - safety chain
  - trailer brake release.

Part Four

Retesting for disqualified drivers

This part looks at what is required when being tested after disqualification.

The topics covered

- New Drivers Act
- The extended test.

New Drivers Act

Who is affected

Special rules apply for the first two years after the date of passing your driving test.

How you may be affected

Your licence will be revoked if the number of penalty points on your licence reaches six or more as a result of offences you commit before the two years are over. This includes offences you committed before passing your test.

You must then reapply for a provisional licence. You may drive only as a learner until you pass the theory and practical driving test again.

This applies even if you pay by fixed penalty.

Penalties

Tough penalties exist for anyone convicted of dangerous driving offences.

Courts must

- impose an extended driving test on anyone convicted of dangerous driving offences.

Courts can also

- impose an extended driving test on anyone convicted of other offences involving obligatory disqualification

- order a normal-length test for other endorsable offences before the disqualified driver can recover a full licence.

Applying for a retest

A driver subject to a retest can apply for a provisional licence at the end of the disqualification period.

The normal rules for provisional licence-holders apply.

The driver must be supervised by a person who

- has held a full EC/EEA driving licence for at least three years and still holds one for the category of the vehicle being driven

- is at least 21 years of age.

The vehicle must display L-plates (or, if you wish, D-plates in Wales) to the front and rear.

Driving on motorways isn't allowed.

The theory test

You will have to pass the theory test before an application for the practical test is accepted.

Details of the theory test can be found in Part One.

Longer and more demanding

The extended test takes about 70 minutes and covers a wide variety of roads, usually including dual carriageways. This test is more demanding. Make sure that you are ready.

You are advised to take suitable instruction from an ADI.

Higher fees

The higher fee reflects the longer duration of the test.

How your examiner will test you

Your test will include all the exercises included in the normal test. Your examiner will watch you and take account of

- your ability to concentrate for the duration of the test
- your attitude to other road users.

Part Five
Further information

This part offers further information.

The topics covered

- If you pass
- The Pass Plus scheme
- If you don't pass
- Officially recommended syllabus
- DSA complaints guide for test candidates
- DSA compensation code for test candidates
- DSA offices and other useful addresses.

If you pass

Well done! You will have shown that you can drive safely.

You will be given

- a pass certificate (D10, or a D10E in the case of an extended test)
- a copy of the driving test report which will show any driving faults which have been marked during the test
- some general guidance to explain your driving test report.

Look at the report carefully and discuss it with your instructor. It will include notes to help you understand how the examiner marks the form. You may then find it helpful to refer to the relevant sections in this book to help you overcome any weaknesses in your driving.

Remember: under the New Drivers Act your licence could be revoked if you receive six or more penalty points within two years of passing your test – see page 61.

Developing your driving standards

You should aim to raise your standard of driving with additional instruction and experience.

The Pass Plus scheme has been developed by the Department of the Environment, Transport and the Regions, in partnership with the insurance industry, to enable you to gain experience safely. Your instructor may have details, or you may contact DSA on 0115 901 2633 for the names of instructors operating in your area.

There are also other organisations that offer driving courses. Your local Road Safety Officer should be able to supply details.

Motorway driving

It is important that you understand the rules and regulations of the motorway. Your ADI will be able to assist you with gaining some experience before you drive on your own. This will help you to gain the confidence you will need to drive on a busy motorway.

Ask your ADI for lessons in motorway driving.

You will have to pay for the course but, if you complete it successfully, you will be offered a discount on your car insurance by one of the companies taking part in the scheme. The precise saving will depend on the company you choose.

Fees for the Pass Plus course will vary depending on where you live and the instructor or driving school you choose.

By choosing to take part in the scheme you will have shown that you want to be a skilful and responsible driver.

Pass Plus

Pass Plus is a training scheme linked to insurance discounts that will benefit you, the **newly qualified driver** by

- saving you money on your car insurance premiums
- showing you a positive driving style which is both enjoyable and safe
- helping you to gain quality driving experience safely.

The Pass Plus scheme has been developed by the Department of the Environment, Transport and the Regions with the help of insurers and the driver instruction industry. The scheme has been developed to

- improve your skills in areas where you may have little experience
- reduce your risk of being involved in a road accident.

To find out more about the Pass Plus scheme and ADIs in your area telephone 0115 901 2633.

The aim of the Pass Plus scheme

The Pass Plus scheme will

- speed up the process of gaining good driving experience
- teach you positive driving skills.

Throughout the course you will be driving with two key factors in mind

Attitude

- Responsibility for your actions.
- Care and consideration for others.

Skills

- Observation.
- Assessing what you see.
- Making decisions.
- Taking the right action.

Your instructor will tell you why they are the key to a **positive driving** style.

If you don't pass

Your driving isn't up to the standard required. You made mistakes which could have caused danger on the road.

Your examiner will help you by

- giving you a driving test report form. This will show all the faults marked during the test
- explaining briefly why you haven't passed.

Listen to your examiner carefully. She or he will be able to help you by pointing out the aspects of your driving which you need to improve.

Study the driving test report. It will include notes to help you understand how the examiner marks the form. You may then find it helpful to refer to the relevant sections in this book.

Show your copy of the report to your ADI, who will advise and help you to correct the faults. Listen to your ADI's advice carefully and get as much practice as you can.

Right of appeal

You will obviously be disappointed if you don't pass your driving test. Although your examiner's decision can't be changed, if you think your test wasn't carried out according to the regulations, you have the right to appeal.

If you live in England and Wales you have six months after the issue of the Statement of Failure in which to appeal (Magistrates' Courts Act 1952 Ch. 55 part VII, Sect. 104).

If you live in Scotland you have 21 days in which to appeal (Sheriff Court, Scotland Act of Sederunt (Statutory Appeals) 1981).

Driving is a life skill. It will take you many years to acquire the skills set out here to a high standard.

This syllabus lists the skills in which you must achieve basic competence in order to pass the driving test. You must also have

* a thorough knowledge of *The Highway Code* and motoring laws
* a thorough understanding of your responsibilities as a driver.

This means that you must have real concern, not just for your own safety, but for the safety of all road users, including pedestrians and others who are vulnerable.

Make sure that your instructor covers the syllabus fully.

Legal requirements

To learn to drive you must

1. Be at least 17 years old. If you receive the higher mobility component of the Disability Living Allowance (DLA) for a disability you may start driving at 16.

2. Be able to read in good daylight (with glasses or contact lenses, if you wear them) a motor vehicle number plate

- 20.5 metres (about 67 feet) away.
- with letters 79.4 mm (3.1 in.) high. Number plates with a narrower font, such as the new style number plates introduced during 2001, should be read from a distance of 20 metres (66 feet).

3. Be medically fit to drive.

4. Hold a provisional driving licence or full licence for another category (see leaflet D100).*

5. Ensure that the vehicle being driven

- is legally roadworthy
- has a current test certificate if it's over the prescribed age
- displays a valid tax disc.

6. Make sure that the vehicle is properly insured for its use.

7. Display L-plates (or, if you wish, D-plates in Wales) to the front and rear of the vehicle.

8. Be supervised by a person who

- has held (and still holds) a full EC/EEA licence for the category of vehicle driven for at least three years
- is at least 21 years old.

9. Wear a seat belt, unless granted an exemption, and see that all the seat belts in the vehicle and their anchorages and fitting are free from obvious defects.

10. Ensure that children under 14 years are suitably restrained by the appropriate restraint or an adult seat belt.

11. Be aware of the legal requirements to notify medical conditions which could affect safe driving. If a vehicle has been adapted for a disability, ensure that all the adaptations are suitable to control the vehicle safely.

12. Know the rules on the issue, presentation or display of

- driving licences
- insurance certificates
- tax discs.

* Leaflet D100 contains general information on driver licensing and is free from the DVLA or post offices.

Car controls, equipment and components

You must

1. Understand the function of the

- accelerator
- clutch
- gears
- footbrake
- handbrake
- steering

and be able to use these competently.

2. Know the function of other controls and switches in the car that have a bearing on road safety, and use them competently.

3. Understand the meaning of the gauges and other displays on the instrument panel.

4. Know the legal requirements for the vehicle.

5. Be able to carry out routine safety checks such as

- oil and coolant levels
- tyre pressures

and identify defects, especially with the

- steering
- brakes
- tyres
- seat belts
- lights
- reflectors
- direction indicators
- windscreen wipers and washers
- horn
- rear view mirrors
- speedometer
- exhaust system.

6. Understand the effects which a loaded roof rack or extra passengers will have on the handling of your vehicle.

Road user behaviour

You must

1. Know the most common causes of accidents.

2. Know which road users are most at risk and how to reduce that risk.

3. Know the rules, risks and effects of drinking and driving.

4. Know the effect of fatigue, illness and drugs on driving performance.

5. Be aware of any age-related problems among other road users, especially among children, teenagers and the elderly.

6. Be alert and able to anticipate the likely actions of other road users, and be able to take appropriate precautions.

7. Be aware that courtesy and consideration towards other road users are essential for safe driving.

Vehicle characteristics

You must

1. Know the important principles concerning braking distances and road holding under various road and weather conditions.

2. Know the handling characteristics of other vehicles with regard to stability, speed, braking and manoeuvrability.

3. Know that some vehicles are less easily seen than others.

4. Be able to assess the risks caused by the characteristics of other vehicles and suggest precautions that can be taken, for example

- large commercial vehicles pulling to the right before turning left
- blind spots for some commercial vehicle drivers
- bicycles and motorcycles being buffeted by strong winds.

Road and weather conditions

You must

1. Know the particular hazards in both daylight and the dark, and on different types of road, for example

- on single carriageways, including country lanes
- on three-lane roads
- on dual carriageways and motorways.

2. Gain driving experience on urban and higher-speed roads (but not on motorways) in both daylight and the dark.

3. Know which road surfaces provide the better or poorer grip when braking.

4. Know the hazards caused by bad weather, for example

- rain
- fog
- snow
- ice
- strong winds.

5. Be able to assess the risks caused by road and traffic conditions, be aware of how the conditions may cause others to drive unsafely, and be able to take appropriate precautions.

Traffic signs, rules and regulations

You must

1. Have sound knowledge of the meaning of traffic signs and road markings.

2. Have a sound grasp of the meaning of traffic signs, for example

- speed limits
- parking restrictions
- zebra and pelican crossings.

Car control and road procedure

You must have the knowledge and skills to carry out the following tasks safely and competently, practising the proper use of mirrors, observation and signals.

1. Take necessary precautions before getting in or out of the vehicle.

2. Before starting the engine, carry out safety checks on

- doors
- seat and head restraints
- seat belts
- mirrors.

Also check that the handbrake is on and the gear lever is in neutral.

3. Start the engine and move off

- straight ahead and at an angle
- on the level, uphill and downhill.

4. Select the correct road position for normal driving.

5. Use proper observation in all traffic conditions.

6. Drive at a speed suitable for road and traffic conditions.

7. React promptly to all risks.

8. Change traffic lanes.

9. Pass stationary vehicles.

10. Meet, overtake and cross the path of other vehicles.

11. Turn right and left at junctions, including crossroads and roundabouts.

12. Drive ahead at crossroads and roundabouts.

13. Keep a safe separation distance when following other traffic.

14. Act correctly at pedestrian crossings.

15. Show proper regard for the safety of other road users, with particular care towards the most vulnerable.

16. Drive on both urban and rural roads and, where possible, dual carriageways – keeping up with the flow of traffic where it's safe and proper to do so.

17. Comply with traffic regulations and traffic signals given by the police, traffic wardens and other road users.

18. Stop the vehicle safely, normally and in an emergency, without locking the wheels.

19. Turn the vehicle in the road to face the opposite way using the forward and reverse gears.

20. Reverse the vehicle into a side road, keeping reasonably close to the kerb.

21. Park parallel to the kerb while driving in a reverse gear.

22. Park the vehicle in a multi-storey car park or other parking bay, on the level, uphill and downhill, both in forward and reverse directions.

23. Cross all types of railway level crossing.

Additional knowledge

You must know

1. The importance of correct tyre pressures.

2. The action needed to avoid and correct skids.

3. How to drive through floods and flooded areas.

4. What to do if you are involved in an accident or breakdown, including the special arrangements for accidents or breakdowns on a motorway.

5. Basic first aid for use on the road as set out in *The Highway Code*.

6. The action to take to deter car thieves.

Motorway driving

You must gain a sound knowledge of the special rules, regulations and driving techniques for motorway driving before taking your driving test.

After passing your test, lessons are recommended with an ADI before driving unsupervised on motorways.

Towing large trailers or caravans

You must pass a category B theory and practical test before towing a trailer. This will entitle you to tow

- a trailer not exceeding 750 kg
- a larger trailer, where the combination weight of the towing vehicle and the trailer doesn't exceed 3.5 tonnes, and provided the laden weight of the trailer doesn't exceed the unladen weight of the towing vehicle.

Further information is explained in DVLA factsheet INF 30 'Towing Trailers in Great Britain'.

Category B + E allows vehicles up to 3.5 tonnes to be combined with a trailer in excess of 750 kg, where the combination doesn't fall within the definition of category B alone. In order to gain this entitlement, category B licence-holders have to pass a further practical test for B + E.

Whilst learning to drive a category B + E combination, you must comply with the requirements of a provisional licence. The requirements are listed in the first section of the syllabus. In particular, you should note the need to

- display L-plates (or, if you wish, D-plates in Wales) to the front and rear of the unit
- be supervised by a person who is at least 21 years old and has held (and still holds) a full licence for category B + E.

You must achieve everything in the previous sections of this syllabus except items which clearly don't apply to you. In particular, you should know how to

1. Turn a vehicle and trailer to travel in the opposite direction without reversing, where possible. For example, using a roundabout or side roads.

2. Stop the vehicle and trailer as quickly as possible, with safety and under full control.

3. Reverse the towing vehicle and trailer

- under control
- with effective observation
- on a predetermined course
- to enter a restricted opening
- to stop so that the extreme rear of the trailer is within a clearly defined area.

4. Select a safe and suitable place to stop the vehicle and trailer reasonably close to the nearside kerb when required

- on the level
- facing uphill
- facing downhill
- before reaching a parked vehicle, but leaving sufficient room to move away again.

5. Use additional mirrors and observation to compensate for the restricted view caused by large trailers and caravans.

6. Show consideration for other road users by pulling up safely, when necessary, to avoid the build-up of queues of following traffic.

7. Uncouple and recouple the trailer from the towing vehicle safely.

Uncoupling

You must

- select a safe place with firm and level ground
- ensure that the brakes are applied on both the towing vehicle and the trailer
- ensure that the wheels, legs or other devices provided for supporting the trailer after uncoupling are lowered correctly, and that strong planks or metal load spreaders are used to distribute the weight if there is any risk
- disconnect the electric line(s) and stow them away safely
- remove any chain or coupling and manoeuvre the trailer clear of the towing hook
- remove any fitted stabilising equipment and the trailer number plate, where appropriate.

Recoupling

You must

- ensure that the brakes are correctly applied on the trailer
- manoeuvre the towing vehicle so that the trailer may be safely and easily coupled to it
- attach the vehicle to the towing vehicle securely
- attach any safety chain or device and the electrical connections
- correctly fit any stabilising equipment
- connect the electric line(s)
- ensure that the wheels, legs or other devices provided for supporting the trailer are raised and secured correctly
- check that the coupling is secure by using a method appropriate to the vehicle and trailer
- check the operation of all lights and the fitting of the correct number plate, where appropriate
- release the trailer brake, having ensured that the handbrake on the towing vehicle is on.

DSA aims to give its customers the best possible service. Please tell us

- when we have done well
- when you aren't satisfied.

Your comments can help us to improve the service we offer. For information about DSA service standards, contact DSA Test Enquiries and Booking Centre 0870 01 01 372.

If you have any questions about how your test was conducted, please contact the local Supervising Examiner, whose address is displayed at your local driving test centre.

If you are dissatisfied with the reply or you wish to comment on other matters, you can write to DSA.

If your concern relates to an ADI you should write to

The Registrar of Approved Driving Instructors
Driving Standards Agency
Stanley House
Talbot Street
Nottingham NG1 5GU.

Finally, you can write to

The Chief Executive
Driving Standards Agency
Stanley House
56 Talbot Street
Nottingham NG1 5GU.

None of this removes your right to take your complaint to

- your Member of Parliament, who may decide to raise your case personally with the DSA Chief Executive, the Minister, or the Parliamentary Commissioner for Administration (the Ombudsman), whose name and address is at the back of this book
- a magistrates' court (in Scotland, to the Sheriff of your area) if you believe that your test wasn't carried out according to the regulations.

Before doing this, **you should seek legal advice.**

DSA always aims to keep test appointments, but occasionally we have to cancel a test at short notice. We will refund the test fee, or give you your next test free, in the following circumstances

- if we cancel a test
- if you cancel a test and give us at least ten working days' notice
- if you keep the test appointment but the test doesn't take place or isn't finished, for a reason that isn't your fault or the fault of the vehicle you are using.

We will also compensate you for the money you lost because we cancelled your test at short notice (unless it was for bad weather). For example, we will pay

- the cost of hiring a vehicle for the test, including reasonable travelling time to and from the test centre
- any pay or earnings you lost, after tax and so on (usually for half a day).

We WON'T pay the cost of driving lessons which you arrange linked to a particular test appointment, or extra lessons you decide to take while waiting for a rescheduled test.

How to apply

Please write to the DSA Enquiries and Booking Centre and send a receipt showing hire car charges, or an employer's letter which shows what earnings you lost. If possible, please use the standard form (available from every driving test centre or booking office) to make your claim.

These arrangements don't affect your legal rights.

DSA Test Enquiries and Booking Centre

DSA
PO Box 280
Newcastle-upon-Tyne
NE99 1FP

Tel: 0870 01 01 372

Welsh Speakers: 0870 01 00 372

Minicom: 0870 01 07 372

Fax: 0870 01 02 372

DSA Head Office

Stanley House
56 Talbot Street
Nottingham NG1 5GU

Tel: 0115 901 2500
Fax: 0115 901 2940

Other useful addresses

Approved Driving Instructors' National Joint Council

The Secretary
41 Edinburgh Road
Cambridge CB4 1QR

Tel. & Fax: 01223 359079

DTLR Mobility Advice and Vehicle Information Service (MAVIS)

'O' Wing
MacAdam Avenue
Old Wokingham Road
Crowthorne
Berkshire RG45 6XD

Tel: 01344 661000
Fax: 01344 661066

Driver and Vehicle Licensing Agency (DVLA)

Customer Enquiry Unit
Swansea SA6 7JL

Tel: 0870 240 0009

Driving Instructors' Association

The Secretary
Safety House
Beddington Farm Road
Croydon CR0 4XZ

Tel: 0181 665 5151
Fax: 0181 665 5565

Motor Schools Association of Great Britain Ltd

The General Manager
182A Heaton Moor Road
Stockport
Cheshire SK4 4DU

Tel: 0161 443 1611
Fax: 0161 443 1699

Association of Driving Instructors Business Club

3 Greenacre Close
Wyke
Bradford
West Yorkshire
BD12 9DQ

Tel: 01274 672850

Office of the Parliamentary Commissioner for Administration (The Parliamentary Ombudsman)

Millbank Tower
Millbank
London SW1P 4QP

Tel: 020 7217 4163
Fax: 020 7217 4160

Essential guidance

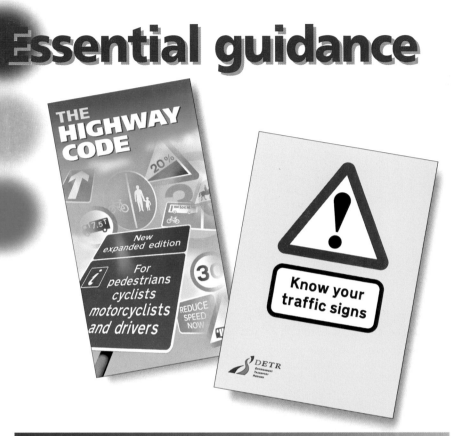

The Highway Code

The Highway Code is essential reading for everyone. It explains road traffic law and gives guidance as to best driving practice, with particular reference to vulnerable road users such as horse riders, cyclists and the elderly. The current version was prepared to reflect the changes in lifestyle and technology, giving rules for dealing with driver fatigue and recommendations about the use of mobile phones.

0 11 552290 5   £1.49

Know Your Traffic Signs

This useful publication illustrates and explains the vast majority of traffic signals, signs and road markings which any road user is likely to encounter.

It is the most comprehensive explanation of road signs available, and is exceptional value for money.

0 11 551612 3   £2.50

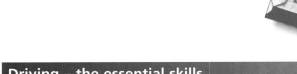

Driving – the essential skills

Successor to *The Official Driving Manual*. An essential reference manual for all motorists and instructors, from learners to advanced motorists – includes the very latest advice and legislation on good driving, covering subjects as diverse as defensive driving, bends and junctions, manoeuvring, towing and European driving, plus legal information.

0 11 552224 7   £12.99

The Official Guide to Accompanying L-Drivers

Understand what a learner driver needs to practice, and be aware of the potential hazards encountered in accompanying a learner driver. This new title ensures that the efforts of others complement the lessons given by their Approved Driving Instructor.

0 11 552178 X   £7.49

Owning a Car

This is the only book on the market that guides the prospective car owner through the minefield of legislation, testing and finance for new and used cars. It is also a guide to the website information on each of the topics covered, from photo-card licences to importing a vehicle, and from exhaust emissions to how to help prevent car theft.

0 11 552214 X   £9.99

Printed in The United Kingdom for the Stationery Office TN008963 12/01 C150 63789

Order Form

5 easy ways to order:

- ● **Online:**   Visit www.**clicktso**.com
- ○ **Tel:**   Please call 0870 600 5522 *quoting ref BFH*
- ● **Fax:**   Fax this form to **0870 600 5533**
- ● **Post:**   **The Stationery Office, PO Box 29, Norwich NR3 1GN**
- ○ **TSO Bookshops:** Visit your local The Stationery Office Bookshop

Please send me the following publications:

Title	ISBN	Price	Quantity
The Highway Code	0 11 552290 5	£1.49	....
Know Your Traffic Signs	0 11 551612 3	£2.50	....
The Official Guide to Accompanying L-Drivers	0 11 552178 X	£7.49	....
Driving – the essential skills	0 11 552224 7	£12.99	....
Owning A Car	0 11 552214 X	£9.99	....

Handling charge per order: £3.00
Total enclosed: £................

PLEASE COMPLETE IN BLOCK CAPITALS

Name ....

Address ....

....

....

.... Postcode .... | BFH |

☐ I enclose a cheque for £.................... payable to: *'The Stationery Office'*

☐ Please charge to my account with The Stationery Office, No:

....

☐ Please debit my Mastercard/Visa/Amex/Diners/Connect Card Account No.

Signature... Expiry date...................................

☐ Please send me information about relevant products and services from The Stationery Office

We can now also send you updates on your specific area of interest by e-mail. To register, visit **clicktso.com**

7

9

10

11

14

18

20

21

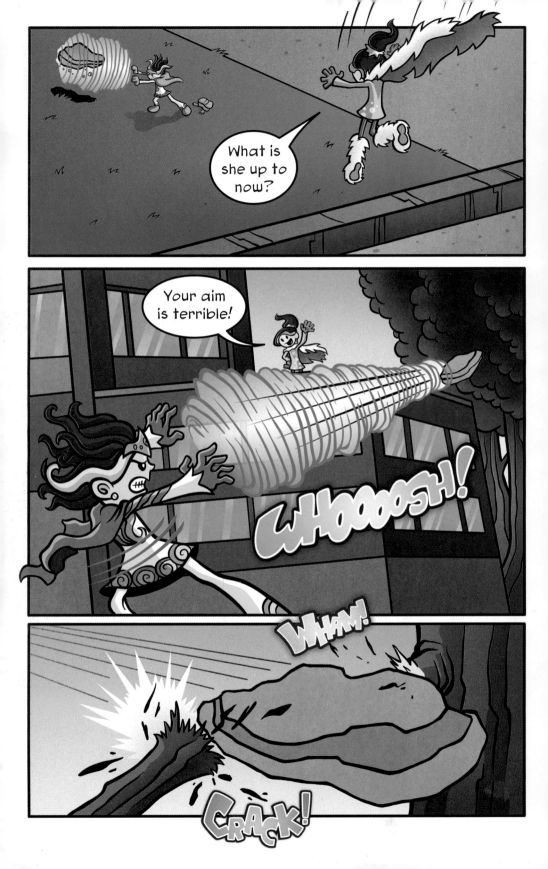

24

25

28

30

31

32

Evil Echo

SUPER-VILLAIN

Villain facts

First appearance
Princess Candy: The Evil Echo

Real name........................Echo Repeater

Occupation................................Student

Height.....................................1.4 metres

Weight..............................34 kilograms

Eyes..............Varies, depending on shape

Hair.................Varies, with green streaks

Special powers
Repetitive speech patterns annoy all who hear her; can shift shape into whoever or whatever she wishes.

Kelly and Kelli Repeater had always dreamed of having twins. So when their daughter Echo was born an only child, they were shattered. To cope with their disappointment, the Repeaters taught Echo to repeat phrases. It made the young parents feel like they had a precious pair rather than a sad singleton. When Echo was five, her parents' dreams finally came true, and Echo had twin brothers. Feeling more alone than ever, Echo discovered she could shift shapes. Now Echo can be a twin to anyone or anything she chooses. She does not hesitate to take over others people's lives, leaving chaos in her path.

AUNT PANDORA'S

PRINCESS PUZZLERS

Q: When were jelly beans invented?

A: In the 1880s.

Q: How long does it take to make a jelly bean?

A: One to three weeks, depending on the flavour.

Q: How many jelly beans are produced in the United States for Easter each year?

A: More than 16 billion. (Jelly beans are connected with Easter in the United States because they look like eggs.)

About The Author

Michael Dahl has written more than 200 books for children and young adults. He is the creator of Princess Candy and author of *Sugar Hero* and *The Marshmallow Mermaid*, two other books in the series.

Scott Nickel works at Paws, inc., Jim Davis's famous Garfield studio. He has written many children's books, including Princess Candy's *The Green Queen of Mean*, *Jimmy Sniffles vs The Mummy* and *Secret of the Summer School Zombies*. Scott lives in Indiana, USA, with his wife, two sons and six cats.

About The Illustrator

Jeff Crowther has been drawing comics for as long as he can remember. Since graduating from college, Jeff has worked on a variety of illustrations for clients including Disney, *Adventures Magazine* and *Boy's Life* magazine. He also wrote and illustrated the webcomic *Sketchbook* and has self-published several mini-comics. Jeff lives in Ohio, USA, with his wife, Elizabeth, and their children, Jonas and Noelle.

Glossary

arctic extremely cold and wintry

funnel cloud a cloud that is wide at the top and narrow at the bottom; funnel clouds sometimes turn into tornadoes

identity who a person is

increase to grow in size or number

magical having power that can make impossible things happen by using charms or spells

obviously in a way that is easy to see or understand

powerful having great strength

strategy clever plan for winning a battle or achieving a goal

ultimate greatest or best

weapon something that can be used in a fight

DISCUSSION QUESTIONS

1. Early in the story, there were clues that Echo was shape-shifting and causing trouble. What were the clues?

2. If you could shift shapes, who or what would you become first? What would you want to do in your new shape? What would be the best part of being someone or something else?

3. Aunt Pandora tells Echo, "Everything you need is inside you." What does this mean? Do you think this is true for yourself?

WRITING PROMPTS

1. In the story, we find out that Echo steals Halo's sweets. Write a story that shows Echo sneaking into Halo's room. How does she do it? What does she see? What is she thinking?

2. You are a journalist who has been asked to write a story about mysterious events at Midnight School. Witnesses spotted two nearly identical girls battling each other. Write your news story.

3. Writers often use character descriptions to develop their characters' personalities and histories. Write a character description for Echo. Include things about her background, hobbies and interests.